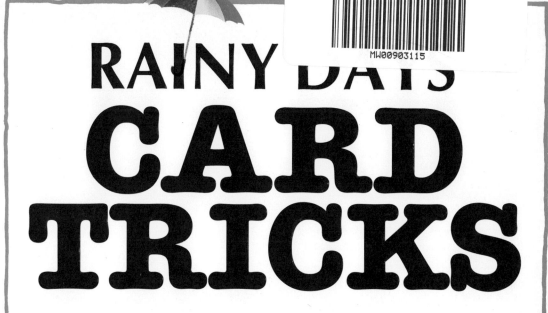

RAINY DAYS
CARD
TRICKS

VANESSA BAILEY

FRANKLIN WATTS
LONDON · NEW YORK · TORONTO · SYDNEY

CONTENTS

Sticky magic	4
Hairy tricks	5
Spot the dot	6
Suit-able trickery	8
Crafty glimpse	10
Copy-cats	12
Card-foolery	14
Burning building	16
Kings and Queens	18
Clever cut	20
Count-down	22
Snap happy	24
Double lift	26
ABRACADABRA	28
Bridge shuffle	30
Sneaky viewing	30
Words to know	32

Design: David West
Children's Book Design
Photography: Roger Vlitos
Editor: Denny Robson
Compiler: Hilary Hosea

© Aladdin Books Ltd 1990

Created and designed by
N.W. Books Ltd
28 Percy Street
London W1P 9FF

First published in
Great Britain in 1990 by
Franklin Watts Ltd
96 Leonard Street
London EC2A 4RH

ISBN 0-7496-0217-1 (hardback)
0-7496-0666-5 (paperback)

A CIP catalogue record for this book
is available from the British Library

Printed in Belgium

Introduction

Many great twentieth century magicians have been famous for their card tricks. Houdini, the great escapologist, called himself the "King of Cards". The card magician Cardini learned his skills in the freezing trenches of the First World War, where he had to practise in gloves. Later he was famous for producing fan after fan of cards on-stage, decked out in white gloves.

This book shows how you too can become a card magician. It shows you how to handle the cards and learn a variety of tricks. As with all kinds of magic, presentation is very important if you want to put on a good show. You will need to rehearse the tricks and the secret moves so that they become smooth and convincing. It also helps to act out the magician's part. Prepare a good 'patter', the jokes, chat and magic words of the magician, so that you can give a confident performance that will amaze your audience!

Most of the tricks in this book need only one pack of cards. For one of the tricks you will need two packs with differently coloured backs. Decks that have been used before will be easier to handle than new cards. You will also need a soft pencil, some paper, double-sided sticky tape and children's glue.

Sticky magic

This card trick will make you appear a wizard of the deck. You tap a card with a rolled up piece of paper and the card is magically transformed into a completely different card!

The secret of the trick
Although it appears that there is only one card on the table, there are really two cards. Unknown to your audience the rolled paper has a sticky side that removes the top card.

BEFORE YOU START
Make a roll of paper and put some double-sided sticky tape on one side of the roll.

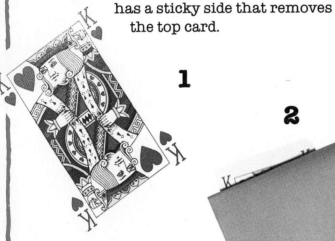

1

2

1 Hold two cards together firmly and show them to your audience as if they were one. The K♥ here is actually on top of the A♠.

2 With some magic words, sharply tap the cards with the sticky roll of paper.

3 With a flourish, quickly raise the paper roll and put it out of sight behind you, so that the audience can't see the card attached to it. The King has turned into an Ace!

3

4

1

BEFORE YOU START
Make sure you do this
trick on a dark or
patterned surface so that
the hair does not show.
Take a dark hair and glue
it to the Ace.

1 Lay out six cards as
shown.

2

3 Point to your hidden
card. The hair will just
be visible, but no one will
be able to guess how
you did it!

3

2 Challenge your
audience to cover the
three cards and
rearrange them while
you turn your back.

Hairy tricks

In this trick you correctly identify your card
after it has been hidden and rearranged by the
audience – and you don't even touch the cards!

The secret of the trick
The secret is very simple. You have attached a
dark hair to the chosen card that no one notices
except you.

Spot the dot

Many of the tricks in this book involve the card magician in mysteriously identifying a card chosen by a member of the audience. In each case the presentation and method are different, so that what the audience actually sees is a wide variety of exciting tricks. This is one of the more simple examples.

The secret of the trick

The secret here is that there is a pencil line along the side of the deck of cards. It will not be noticed by the audience, but it allows you to identify the chosen card.

BEFORE YOU START
Draw a line across the side of the deck of cards as shown. Use a soft pencil as this will make a wide mark and it will be easily erased.

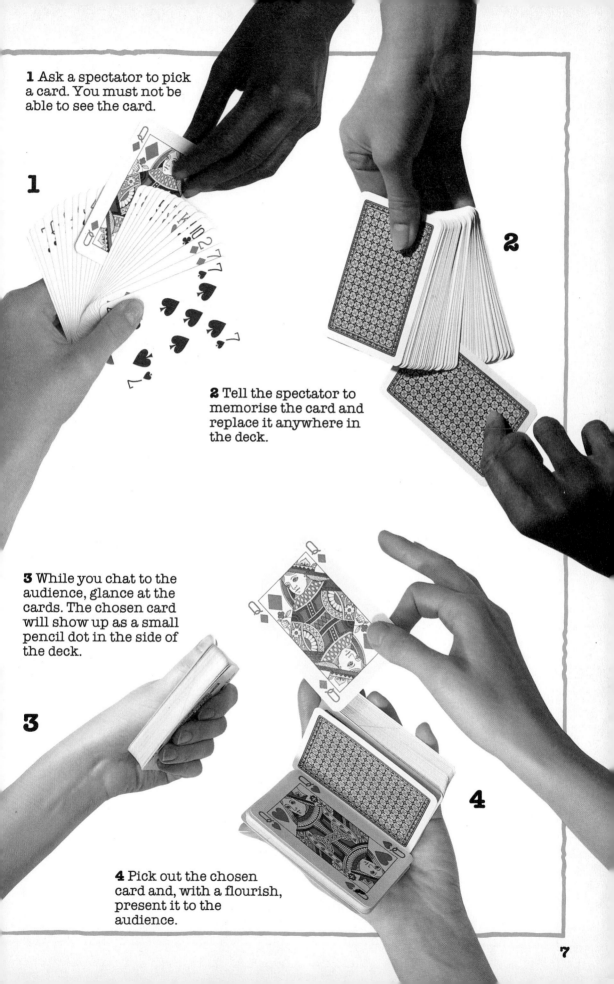

1 Ask a spectator to pick a card. You must not be able to see the card.

1

2

2 Tell the spectator to memorise the card and replace it anywhere in the deck.

3 While you chat to the audience, glance at the cards. The chosen card will show up as a small pencil dot in the side of the deck.

3

4

4 Pick out the chosen card and, with a flourish, present it to the audience.

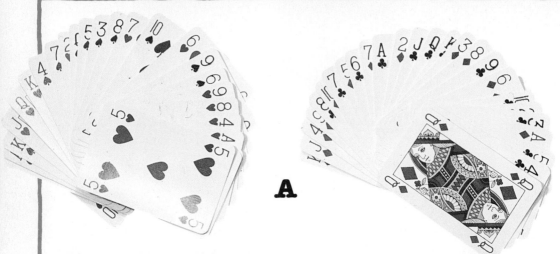

A

Suit-able trickery

In this trick you astonish your audience once
more by finding a card that was chosen and then
replaced at random in the pack.

The secret of the trick

What the spectators don't realise is that you
have carefully prepared the pack in advance so
that the replacement of the chosen card is not as
random as it seems.

**BEFORE YOU
START (A)**
Sort the pack into two
halves, one containing
spades and hearts, the
other with diamonds an
clubs. The audience wil
not notice this
arrangement because
the cards will still be a
mixture of blacks and
reds.

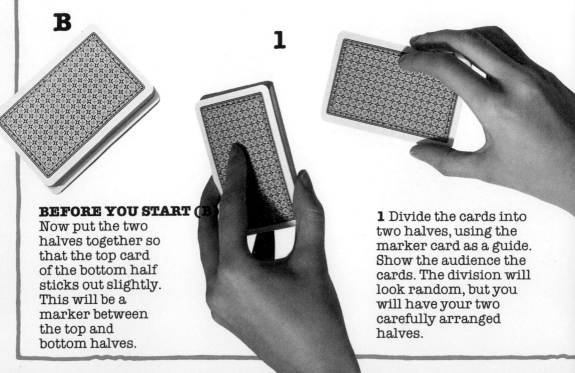

B

1

BEFORE YOU START (B)
Now put the two
halves together so
that the top card
of the bottom half
sticks out slightly.
This will be a
marker between
the top and
bottom halves.

1 Divide the cards into
two halves, using the
marker card as a guide.
Show the audience the
cards. The division will
look random, but you
will have your two
carefully arranged
halves.

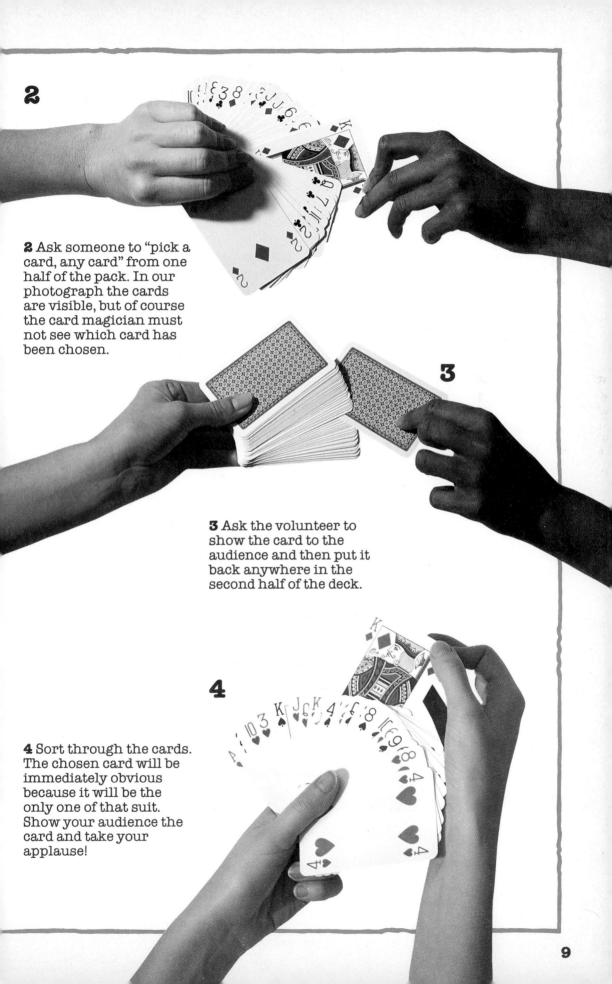

2

2 Ask someone to "pick a card, any card" from one half of the pack. In our photograph the cards are visible, but of course the card magician must not see which card has been chosen.

3

3 Ask the volunteer to show the card to the audience and then put it back anywhere in the second half of the deck.

4

4 Sort through the cards. The chosen card will be immediately obvious because it will be the only one of that suit. Show your audience the card and take your applause!

Crafty glimpse

This trick shows another way of identifying a card chosen and replaced by your audience. Once you have perfected this simple method, you can use it to make up your own card tricks.

The secret of the trick

The secret of this trick is that you have taken a crafty glimpse at the bottom card while your audience's attention was elsewhere. By arranging the cards in a particular way, this glimpse enables you to identify the chosen card.

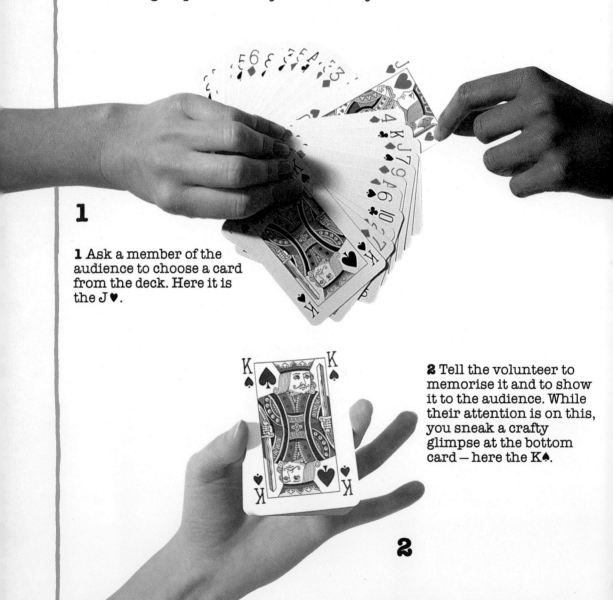

1

1 Ask a member of the audience to choose a card from the deck. Here it is the J ♥.

2 Tell the volunteer to memorise it and to show it to the audience. While their attention is on this, you sneak a crafty glimpse at the bottom card — here the K♠.

2

3

3 Ask the volunteer to put the card back on the top of the deck face downwards.

4 As you chat to the audience, casually cut the pack at random.

4

5 Tap the cards, say some magic words and then sort through the pack. The chosen card will be under the crafty glimpse card. Present it to your audience!

5

Copy-cats

You need two packs of differently coloured cards for this trick.

In this impressive trick, the card magician appears to be a mindreader! Using two packs of cards, you pick out a card that is the same as the card secretly chosen by a spectator.

The secret of the trick
The trick is actually very simple. It all relies on the 'crafty glimpse' method.

1 Give a pack of cards to a member of the audience and tell him to copy everything you do. Shuffle the cards.

2 While the volunteer is busy with his shuffling, sneak a crafty glimpse at the bottom card of your deck.

3

3 In the photographs the bottom card is the J♥. Now swap cards with the volunteer.

4

4 Ask the volunteer to pick a card from his deck. Tell him you are going to read his mind and that you will pick the same card. Pick any card but do not let him see.

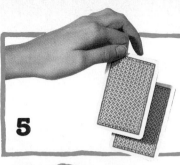

5 Replace your chosen card on the top of your pack of cards and tell the volunteer to do the same.

5

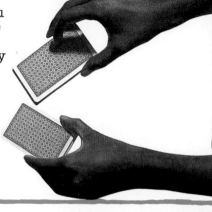

6 Remember that you know the card on the bottom of his pack because of your crafty glimpse earlier. Now both cut your cards.

6

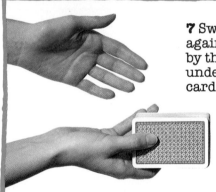

7 Swap decks of cards again. The card chosen by the spectator will be under the crafty glimpse card in your pack.

7

8 Tell the volunteer to pick out the chosen card from his pack and place it on the table. Pick out the card which is under the crafty glimpse card.

9 Turn over the cards. You must have read his mind!

8

9

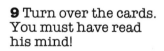

1 Ask a spectator to choose a card.

Card-foolery

This trick is a jokey version of the 'pick a card' trick. Just when the audience is convinced that your trick has failed, you miraculously turn over the chosen card.

The secret of the trick

This is another trick that uses the crafty glimpse method, but what makes it distinctive is that you fool your audience into thinking that you are doing it all wrong!

2 While the spectator memorises the card and shows it to the audience, you glance at the bottom card.

3 Ask the spectator to place his or her card face down on the top of the deck.

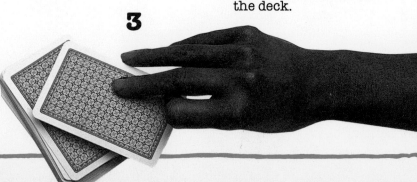

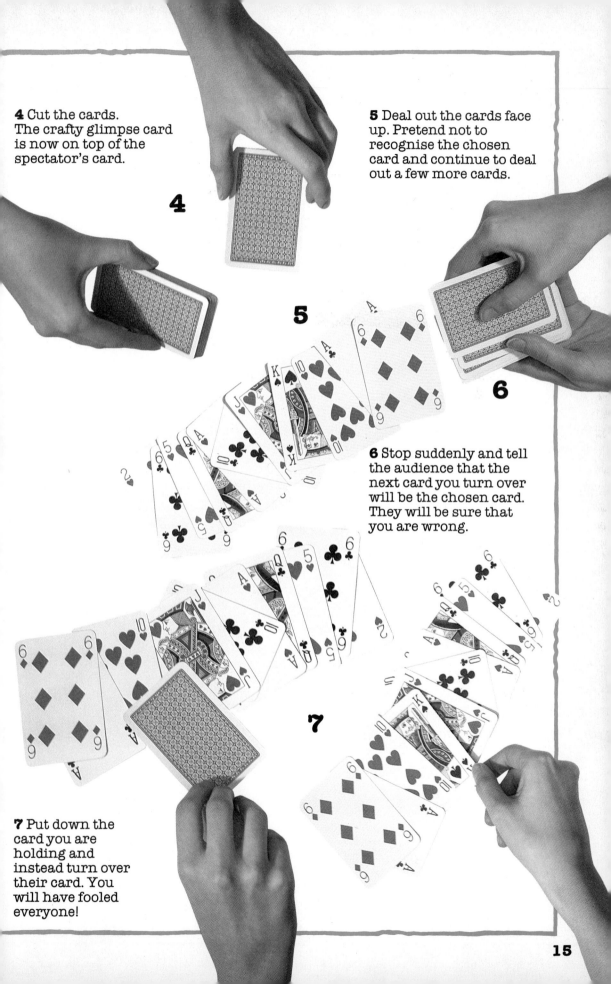

4 Cut the cards. The crafty glimpse card is now on top of the spectator's card.

4

5 Deal out the cards face up. Pretend not to recognise the chosen card and continue to deal out a few more cards.

5

6

6 Stop suddenly and tell the audience that the next card you turn over will be the chosen card. They will be sure that you are wrong.

7

7 Put down the card you are holding and instead turn over their card. You will have fooled everyone!

A

BEFORE YOU START (A)
Rehearse your story so that you can give a confident presentation. Pick out the two red Kings, black Queens, red Jacks and one ten.

Burning building

This trick is great fun to do. It involves a story which you act out with the cards. Members of a royal family escape from a burning building and miraculously they move from the middle to the bottom of the pack.

The secret of the trick

This crafty trick relies on a little preparation of the deck before your audience arrives.

1 Explain to your audience that the deck is the royal building. The King lives at the top of the building. Place the K♥ in the deck near the top.

1

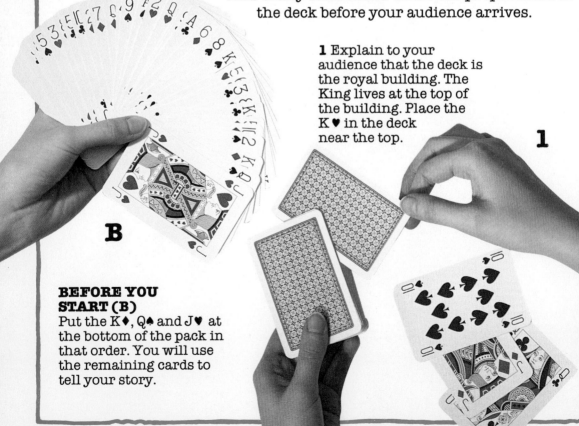

B

BEFORE YOU START (B)
Put the K♦, Q♠ and J♥ at the bottom of the pack in that order. You will use the remaining cards to tell your story.

2 The Queen lives on the next floor down. Place the Q♣ halfway down.

3 The Jack lives on the floor below this. Place the J♦ near the bottom.

4 The servant — the 10♠ — lives right at the bottom. Put this card on the bottom of the pack. Tell the audience how a fire breaks out in the building.

5 Luckily there is a fire escape and the family is able to descend to the street. Turn over the royal cards at the bottom of the deck. Your audience will be amazed!

2

3

4

5

Kings and Queens

This is another trick which involves the telling of a tale, this time of coaches and a royal ball. A King and Queen which are carefully put into one group, strangely turn up in another!

The secret of the trick
The secret here is that you perform a secret move, a 'sleight-of-hand', while your audience's attention is focused elsewhere.

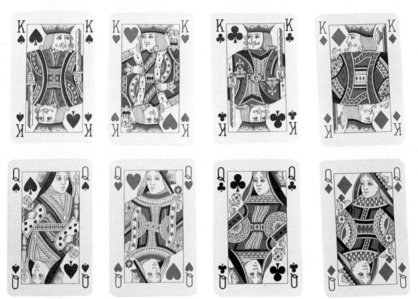

BEFORE YOU START
Take out the Kings and Queens from the pack. Rehearse a story to go with the trick for a really good performance.

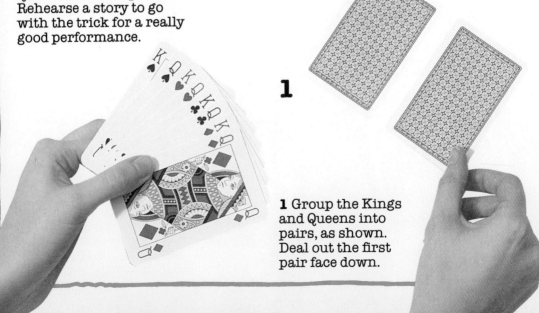

1

1 Group the Kings and Queens into pairs, as shown. Deal out the first pair face down.

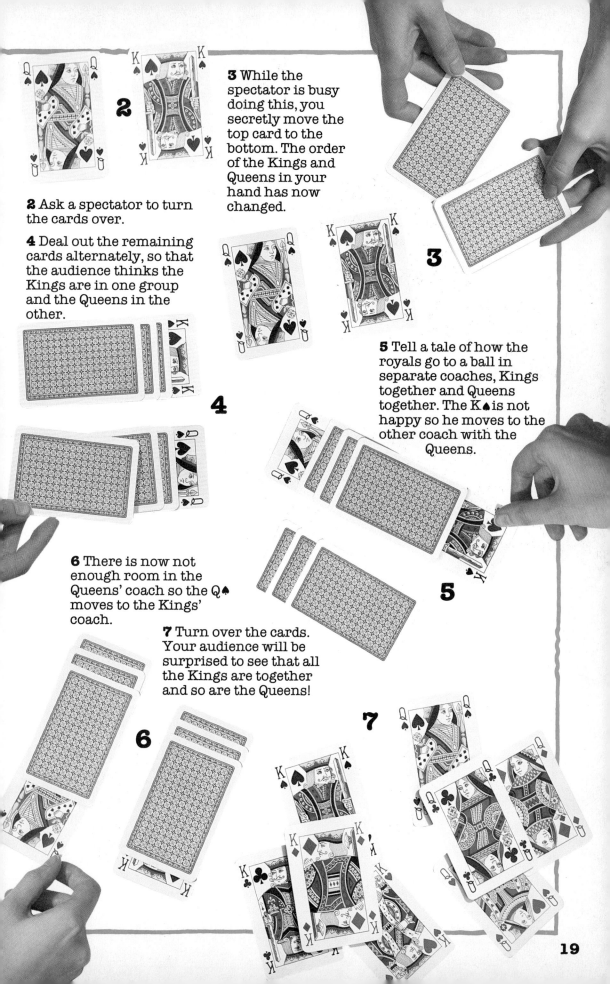

2

2 Ask a spectator to turn the cards over.

4 Deal out the remaining cards alternately, so that the audience thinks the Kings are in one group and the Queens in the other.

4

3 While the spectator is busy doing this, you secretly move the top card to the bottom. The order of the Kings and Queens in your hand has now changed.

3

5 Tell a tale of how the royals go to a ball in separate coaches, Kings together and Queens together. The K♠ is not happy so he moves to the other coach with the Queens.

5

6 There is now not enough room in the Queens' coach so the Q♠ moves to the Kings' coach.

7 Turn over the cards. Your audience will be surprised to see that all the Kings are together and so are the Queens!

6

7

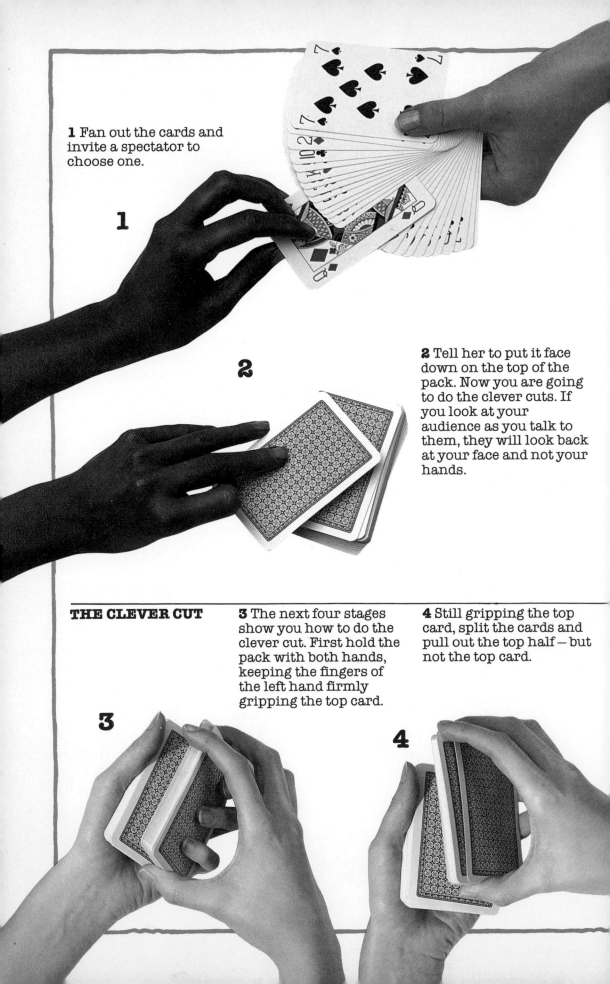

1 Fan out the cards and invite a spectator to choose one.

1

2

2 Tell her to put it face down on the top of the pack. Now you are going to do the clever cuts. If you look at your audience as you talk to them, they will look back at your face and not your hands.

THE CLEVER CUT

3 The next four stages show you how to do the clever cut. First hold the pack with both hands, keeping the fingers of the left hand firmly gripping the top card.

4 Still gripping the top card, split the cards and pull out the top half — but not the top card.

3

4

Clever cut

In this trick a spectator places her chosen card on the top of the deck and no matter how many times you cut the pack, the card magically remains at the top!

The secret of the trick
The magic here is created by handling the cards in a such way that the cuts appear genuine, but they leave the top card in the same position. You will need to practise this well to be convincing.

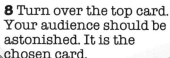

8 Turn over the top card. Your audience should be astonished. It is the chosen card.

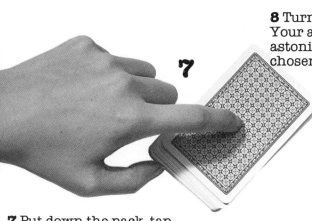

7 Put down the pack, tap it or perhaps say a few magic words.

8

---

5 The chosen card will still be the top card in your left hand.

6 Put the cards that are in your right hand under those in your left. You can repeat the cut several times. The chosen card will always stay on top.

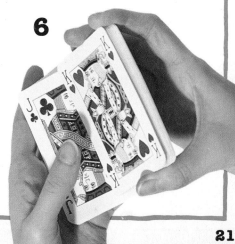

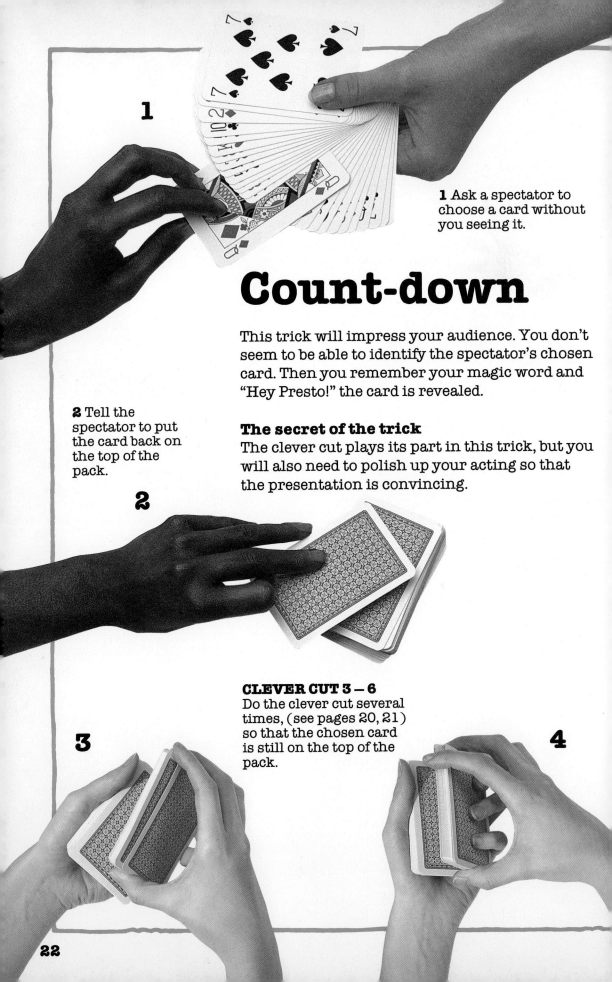

1

1 Ask a spectator to choose a card without you seeing it.

Count-down

This trick will impress your audience. You don't seem to be able to identify the spectator's chosen card. Then you remember your magic word and "Hey Presto!" the card is revealed.

2 Tell the spectator to put the card back on the top of the pack.

The secret of the trick
The clever cut plays its part in this trick, but you will also need to polish up your acting so that the presentation is convincing.

2

CLEVER CUT 3 – 6
Do the clever cut several times, (see pages 20, 21) so that the chosen card is still on the top of the pack.

3

4

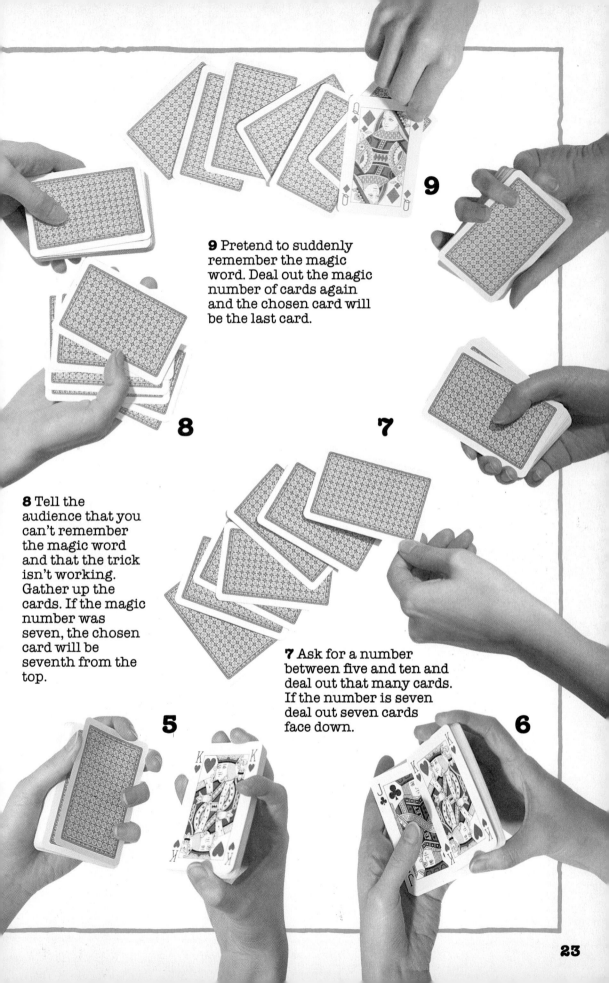

9 Pretend to suddenly remember the magic word. Deal out the magic number of cards again and the chosen card will be the last card.

9

8

7

8 Tell the audience that you can't remember the magic word and that the trick isn't working. Gather up the cards. If the magic number was seven, the chosen card will be seventh from the top.

7 Ask for a number between five and ten and deal out that many cards. If the number is seven deal out seven cards face down.

5

6

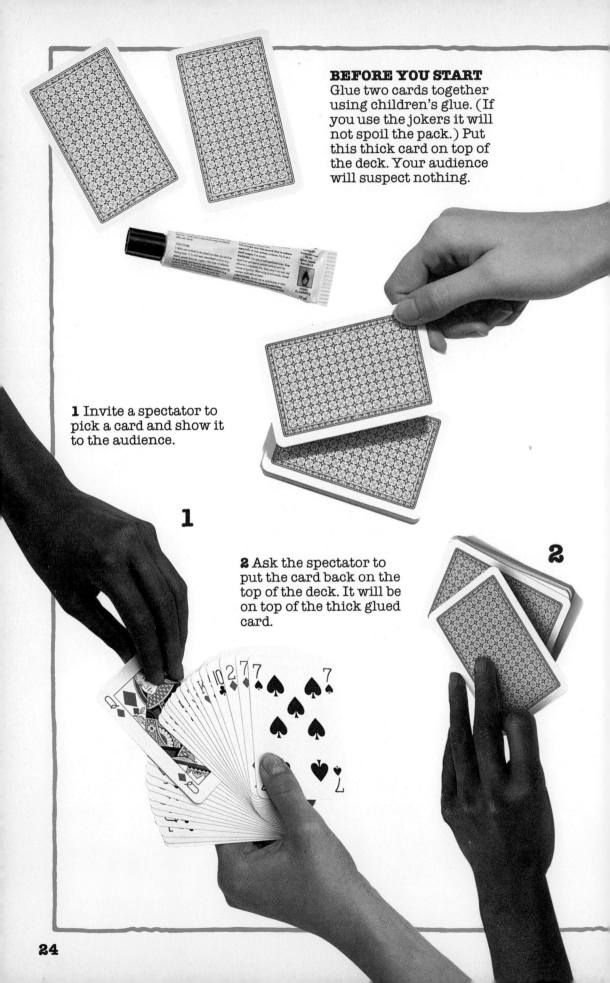

BEFORE YOU START
Glue two cards together using children's glue. (If you use the jokers it will not spoil the pack.) Put this thick card on top of the deck. Your audience will suspect nothing.

1 Invite a spectator to pick a card and show it to the audience.

1

2 Ask the spectator to put the card back on the top of the deck. It will be on top of the thick glued card.

2

Snap happy

This is a wonderfully simple trick in which you identify the card chosen by a member of the audience — without even looking at what the cards are!

The secret of the trick

The secret here relies on some crafty preparation before your audience arrives. Unknown to the spectators, you have glued two cards together. The resulting 'thick' card gives a definite snap when flicked which enables you to identify the chosen card.

3 Cut the cards at random.

4 Flick through the pack until you feel the snap that tells you where the thick glued card is.

5 The chosen card will be the card above the snappy card.

1

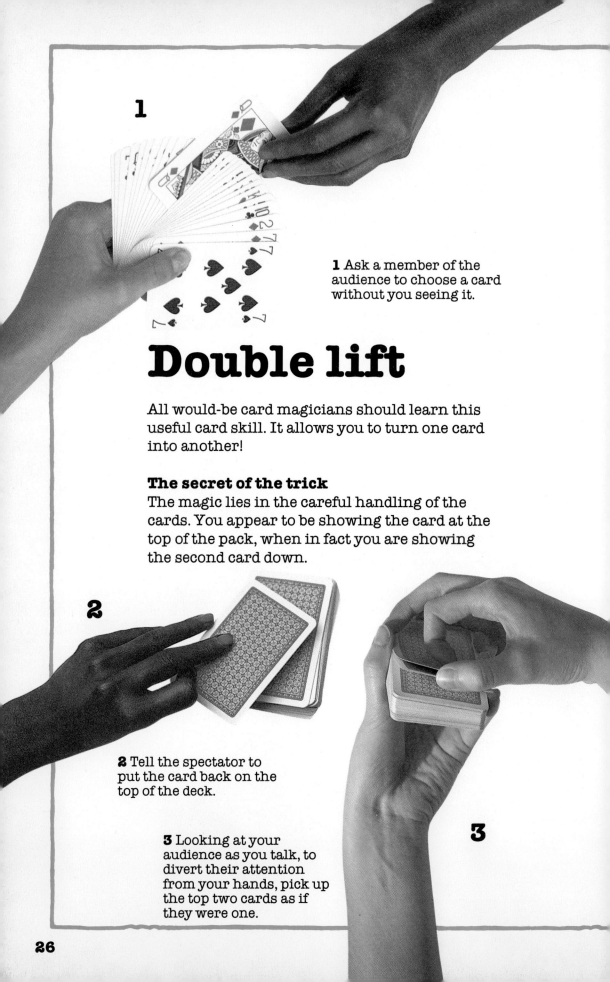

1 Ask a member of the audience to choose a card without you seeing it.

Double lift

All would-be card magicians should learn this useful card skill. It allows you to turn one card into another!

The secret of the trick

The magic lies in the careful handling of the cards. You appear to be showing the card at the top of the pack, when in fact you are showing the second card down.

2

2 Tell the spectator to put the card back on the top of the deck.

3 Looking at your audience as you talk, to divert their attention from your hands, pick up the top two cards as if they were one.

3

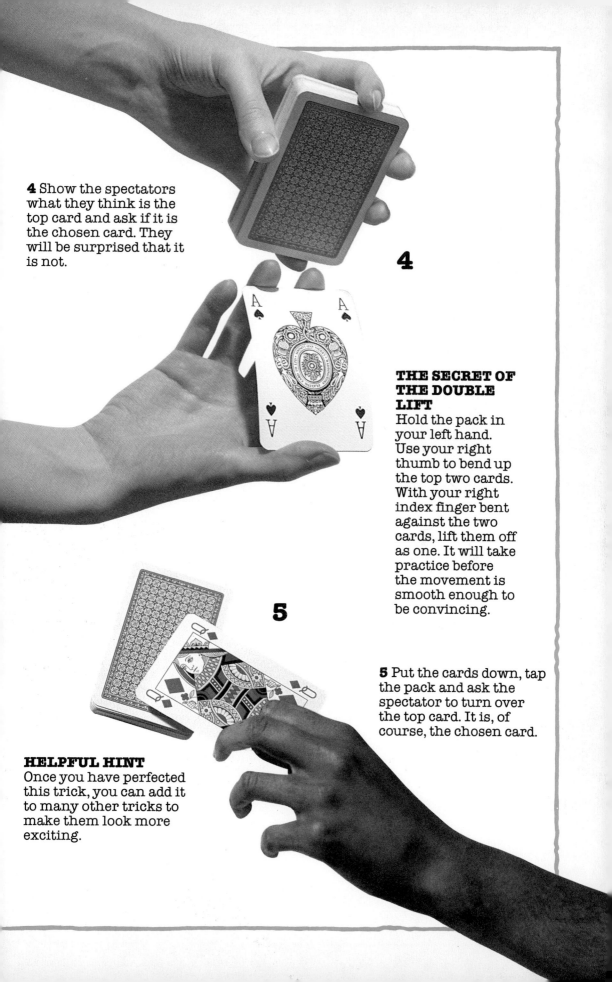

4 Show the spectators what they think is the top card and ask if it is the chosen card. They will be surprised that it is not.

4

THE SECRET OF THE DOUBLE LIFT

Hold the pack in your left hand. Use your right thumb to bend up the top two cards. With your right index finger bent against the two cards, lift them off as one. It will take practice before the movement is smooth enough to be convincing.

5

5 Put the cards down, tap the pack and ask the spectator to turn over the top card. It is, of course, the chosen card.

HELPFUL HINT

Once you have perfected this trick, you can add it to many other tricks to make them look more exciting.

ABRACADABRA

No matter how sharp your spectators are, they will never guess how you identified the chosen card in this clever trick.

The secret of the trick
This trick appears to work all by itself! In fact it relies on a numerical arrangement of the cards, but all the card magician has to remember are the following simple stages.

2 Ask a spectator to choose one of the groups and to memorise one of the cards in it. He or she must not tell you which card it is.

1 Take 21 cards and *alternately* deal out three groups of seven cards.

3 Tell the spectator to replace the group of cards.

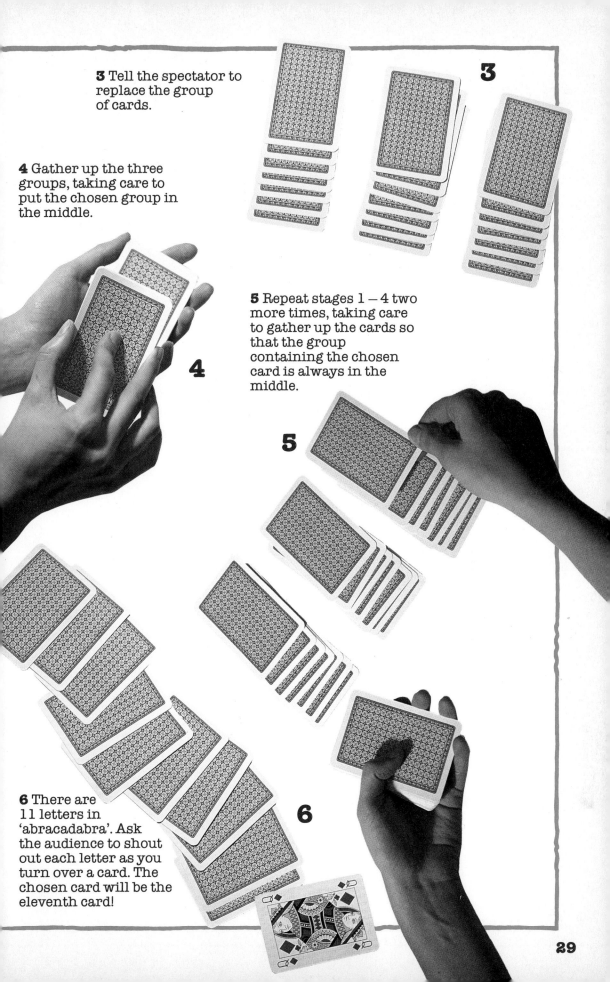

3

4 Gather up the three groups, taking care to put the chosen group in the middle.

4

5 Repeat stages 1 – 4 two more times, taking care to gather up the cards so that the group containing the chosen card is always in the middle.

5

6 There are 11 letters in 'abracadabra'. Ask the audience to shout out each letter as you turn over a card. The chosen card will be the eleventh card!

6

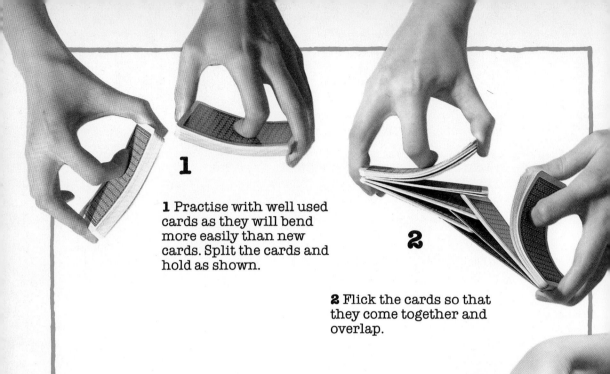

1 Practise with well used cards as they will bend more easily than new cards. Split the cards and hold as shown.

2 Flick the cards so that they come together and overlap.

3 Bend the overlapped cards into a bridge shape, holding your fingers as shown in the photograph.

Bridge shuffle

One of the things you need to learn to become a successful card magician is the art of handling the cards. This only comes with practice, but it is fun to learn. Rehearse fanning out the cards with a smooth gesture for when you invite a spectator to pick a card. Practise shuffling and squaring the pack with quick, deft movements. If you can add the bridge shuffle to your skills, you can be sure of impressing your audience.

4 Slowly release the bridge so that the cards all flick together.